Introduction: Lasting Impressions 2

The Flukey Facts of Fossil Formation 4

Can You Dig It? 6

The Tales Fossils Tell 8

Vanished! Mass Extinction Theories 10

Strange-but-True Stories: Lost
(and Found) Worlds 12

A Closer Look: Trace and True-Form
Fossils 14

Strange-but-True Stories: The World's
Weirdest Fossils 16

The Inside Scoop on Dig Sites 18

The Fossils Around You 20

A Closer Look: Ancient Plants and
Land Animals 22

A Closer Look: Ancient Flying Creatures 26

A Closer Look: Ancient Sea Creatures 30

A Closer Look: Dinosaurs—Big
and Really Small 32

Strange-but-True Stories:
Official State Fossils 38

Greatest Fossil Finds 42

Greatest Fossil Frauds 44

Glossary 46

TABLE OF CONTENTS

Living things leave evidence of their existence. A bird may leave behind a feather as it flies from its perch. A bear will rub off the bark of its favorite scratching tree, leaving pieces of fur behind. You may leave a trail of crumbs on the counter after getting an afternoon snack.

You leave other types of evidence as well. When you walk on the

beach or rest your head on a pillow, you leave an impression—a temporary imprint showing you were there. Someone who would come behind you would know something of you—your size, your weight, and possibly even your age. Nature has given us lasting impressions in the form of **fossils**, a wordless recorded history of our Earth.

Fossils often begin as plants or living creatures that get buried deep under **sediment** (think mud) for long periods of time. The resulting casts, molds, or **petrified** fossils become windows into the ancient world, giving us insight into plant and animal life, behaviors, and even climate.

LASTING IMPRESSIONS

ROCK-HARD FACT

Very few fossils show an entire animal. However, scientists are able to piece together clues on what an animal looked like from looking at multiple fossils, such as this impression of an ancient cousin of the modern armadillo.

BASIC FOSSIL TYPES

Fossils form under a variety of conditions and can show us an image of an entire **organism** or simply provide evidence of its eating habits or other behaviors. Here are the five common types:

1. Mold: an imprint left as an organism dissolves over time

2. Cast: a 3-D replica of an organism resulting from a mold that fills with debris

3. Petrified: an organism whose image is turned to stone as it dissolves and is replaced with **minerals**

4. Trace: footprints, trails, burrows, dung, or other impressions of ancient activity

5. True form: an entirely preserved plant or animal, including soft tissue, a.k.a. guts

Conditions have to be just right for fossils to form, which makes fossils pretty rare birds—or dinosaurs or plants or sea creatures. We'll illustrate with a pterodactyl, an ancient flying dinosaur.

1. **It dies and gets buried really, really fast.** The pterodactyl could have been buried rapidly as the result of an earthquake, volcano, or massive weather event. It could have also been buried in ice or tar. The sediment, ash, ice, or tar would have preserved the dinosaur's bones.

2. **It gets buried deeper over time.** More sediment builds up over the bones. The bones can dissolve over time and leave an imprint (a mold). Sometimes that mold will fill in with minerals (a cast), or minerals may slowly replace the bones, resulting in petrification.

3. **Earth shifts.** Giant plates within the Earth shift and eventually push the pterodactyl fossil back toward the surface.

4. **It's unearthed.** Eventually, **erosion** or **excavation** exposes the pterodactyl fossil hidden beneath the surface.

THE FLUKEY FACTS OF FOSSIL FORMATION

The strata within the earth hold scattered secrets to our planet's history. Within them lies the fossil record or **geologic** column, which documents changes in **climate**, **environment**, life forms, and behaviors over long periods of time. Decoding the fossil record involves scientists who study earth science, life science, **culture**, and physical science.

Fossils help scientists understand how living things have **adapted** over the years. Most of the fossil record is preserved within layers of **sedimentary** rock, which covers about 75 percent of Earth's surface.

By studying which organisms are found within which **strata**, scientists can map out a timeline for how and when life began and how it has changed over time.

There's more to the fossils you see in a museum—or the fossils included with this book—than the fossil formation. There's also fossil excavation, which involves as much art as it does science.

Excavating a dig site can take weeks or even months, and it requires years of training and special tools. Workers have to be able to sense how hard or soft the rock feels beneath their tools so they are careful not to damage **specimens**, and they have to know how to make repairs if damage is done. A specimen as small as a hand can require a year of work to expose.

The work is tricky in many ways. Sometimes **paleontologists**—scientists who study fossils—find a mishmash of bones from many different animals, so they have to try to figure out which bones belong to which animal. Sometimes it's hard to tell rock from bone, which can be easily broken. Once the fossil is unearthed, it is taken to a lab for further study.

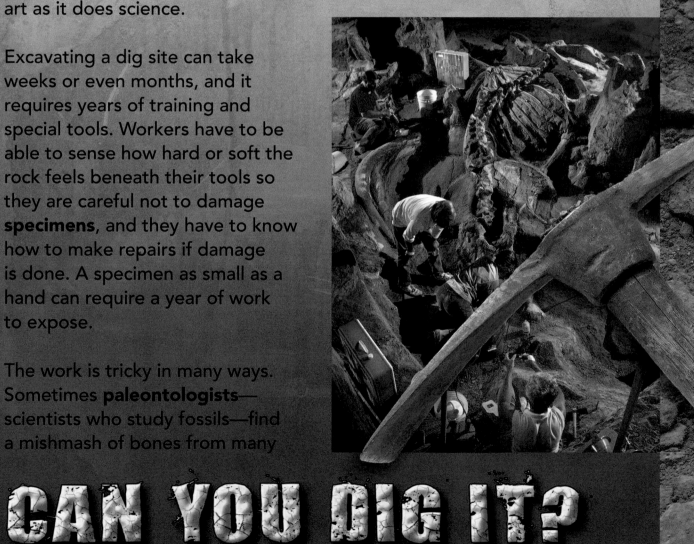

CAN YOU DIG IT?

Paleontologists carry a variety of special tools when excavating sites. The closer they get to the fossil, the more careful they have to be. They begin with shovels and picks. When getting close to bones, they use a rock hammer. Some rock hammers have a chisel edge that chips away gently at sedimentary rock. Next comes a rock knife, then an even smaller knife, and then a pick. Paintbrushes gently sweep away debris. Any bones found are placed in something like a cast to protect them.

Fossils tell a hundred stories without saying a word. They tell us when the first simple life forms appeared on Earth, when plants and trees first emerged, when animals and people appeared, and how life forms have adapted throughout Earth's history. They also help us understand **extinct** animals, such as dinosaurs.

Fossils also tell us about the changes in Earth's **geology** over its history.

From studying fossils of plant life, scientists get a picture of what the climate in an area once was like. Plant fossils can also show what ancient creatures once used for food. They can also tell us where water once covered what is now dry land.

MOSASAUR

CYNOGNATHUS

THE TALES FOSSILS TELL

ROCK-HARD FACT

The branch of science that involves dating rocks and events in Earth's geological history is known as geochronology.

Its meaning is found in its Latin roots: *geo*, meaning "Earth"; and *chronos*, meaning "time." Both geologists and paleontologists must understand geochronology.

THE TICK THAT TALKS TODAY

Inside ancient amber lies a tick with a belly full of blood—but not just any blood. Scientists say it's 20 million-year-old blood that belongs to a **mammal**, possibly a monkey. One theory: as two monkeys were grooming each other, the tick fell into pine tree resin that hardened into amber. A miner found the tick within its amber tomb. It eventually was given to George Poinar Jr., the scientist whose work inspired *Jurassic Park*.

Being a scientist is like being a detective. Scientists can't just look at rock layers and instantly know how old they are. They use two types of dating: relative and absolute. Relative dating is general like saying, "The top rock layer is younger than the one below it." Absolute dating gives an actual age, as if we said that your friend is 9, and your friend's mom is 35.

Rocks and minerals contain **radiation**—like the waves used in an x-ray—contained in **elements** that break down over time. The radioactive elements are like clocks that are set when the rocks form. The amount of the element's breakdown gives scientists an age, usually measured in millions of years.

What caused so many animals to become suddenly extinct? Scientists have many ideas about the global gloom that brought about their doom.

ROCK-HARD FACT

The Permian Period was the deadliest time in Earth's history. Only four of every 100 **species** survived the Permian Period, earning it the nickname the Great Dying. Some of the lost **marine** species are found in the Glass Mountains of Texas, once an underwater reef. The fossils were pushed high above the surface as plates within Earth's crust shifted.

VANISHED!

MASS EXTINCTION THEORIES

- **A KILLER METEORITE:** Scientists have found a crater in Mexico caused by a 6-mile-wide (9.66-km-wide) meteorite that struck Earth around the same time many species went missing from the fossil record. They believe the meteorite caused a worldwide change that killed between 60 and 75 percent of all life on Earth.

- **AN EPIC VOLCANO:** As if a regular volcano weren't epic enough, picture one that spews lava for thousands of years so that the molten rock keeps spreading and killing everything in its path.

- **CLIMATE CHANGE:** Earth's climate has gone through wild changes over time: from hot to cold and wet to dry. In fact, scientists say our planet has gone through several ice ages when ice covered the land. Some organisms can't handle such harsh conditions.

- **DEADLY GAS:** As the climate shifts from cold to warm again, deadly gases that collect in water bodies are released. Some scientists believe a massive amount of deadly gases resulted from climate change, killing off dinosaurs and other ancient species.

THE FROZEN LAST MOMENTS OF POMPEII

The ancient Italian city of Pompeii is lost but not forgotten, remaining an eerie, enduring museum of life—and death. In 79 AD, a massive eruption of Mount Vesuvius blanketed the town in a flood of hot, deadly gas and ash and preserved the last moments of hundreds of petrified humans—people literally frozen in place.

But the people didn't die from the lava or ash. Scientists believe they died instantly from heat under temperatures reaching 570°F (300°C).

STRANGE-BUT-TRUE STORIES: LOST (AND FOUND) WORLDS

AN ANCIENT ASHEN ANIMAL TOMB

The weird nature of the remains in Pompeii have helped scientists solve the mystery of well-preserved animal fossils found within a Chinese lake bed. Just like the petrified people of Pompeii, the bird, dinosaur, and mammal fossils were found in their death poses, but no one knew why until recently.

Scientists finally noted the similarities between the Pompeii fossils and the animal fossils, and they came to a conclusion: the crispy critters died in a massive eruption like the one at Mount Vesuvius.

Just as the preserved fossils and **artifacts** help scientists understand Pompeii's people and culture, the animal fossils will help scientists learn about the area's **ecosystem** during a period when dinosaurs roamed the planet.

ROCK-HARD FACT

Scientists have found an amber window that looks tens of millions of years back in time. Within these tombs of amber lie perfectly preserved lizards who once lived in the tropical forests of what is now Myanmar. Many of the lizards—one of which is an early **ancestor** of chameleons—are fully intact, with scales, tongues, and claws. The **reptiles** will help fill in gaps about adaptations that led to modern-day lizards.

Trace fossils—nests, footprints, or animal droppings—give us clues about how and where an animal lived and moved or even what it ate. Footprints (think dinosaurs) are more common than fossilized dinosaurs, in fact.

Other common trace fossils include animal burrows, trails left behind by sea creatures, bite marks, skin prints, and nests. The existence of trace fossils alert scientists that body fossils may be in the area. They can also shed light on how ancient creatures raised their young or the dangers they faced from nearby **predators.**

FOSSILIZED DINO POO!

Scientists call them **coprolites**, from Greek words that mean "dung stones." They do not smell, and they tell the **paleoscatologists** who study them a whole lot about the creatures that left them behind, like what they ate. Some poo may contain pieces of bone from its **prey.**

A CLOSER LOOK: TRACE AND TRUE-FORM FOSSILS

Only true-form fossils allow scientists to study perfectly preserved organisms. That's because a true-form fossil contains the entire plant or animal. Scientists can see the organism's size, color, and other unique qualities. Most amazing of all is that soft tissue—the skin, the flesh, and the guts—never decay!

Ice, resins such as amber, and tar have proved to be the ultimate antiaging tools. Plants and animals trapped quickly within any of those materials can look exactly the same millions of years later. The cost of such preservation: certain death.

SABER-TOOTHED SQUIRRELS

These are ancient saber-toothed squirrels with teeth long enough to rip your face off. These big-eyed, long-nosed squirrels lived among dinosaurs and, judging from the teeth, ate living things instead of nuts.

FROZEN DINNER AND DINER

If you're afraid of spiders, then maybe it's best not to imagine yourself as a flying insect that has spent 97 million to 110 million years in the clutches of a hungry spider. The frozen-in-place predator and prey have been trapped in amber since dinosaurs roamed Earth.

STRANGE-BUT-TRUE STORIES: THE WORLD'S WEIRDEST FOSSILS

GREAT WHITE SHARK

GIANT ANTS

A 2-in. (5-cm) ant fossil was found in Wyoming, which scientists say had a tropical climate during the ant's lifetime. Scientists believe the ants lived in a period of global warming.

MEGALODON

GINORMOUS JAWS

A fossil hunter put together pieces of an ancient Megalodon shark whose jaw measures 11 ft. (3.4 m) across and 9 ft. (2.7 m) high. Rebuilding the jaw, found in a South Carolina river, took a jaw-dropping 20 years. Scientists say Megalodons measured 52 ft. 6 in. (16 m) long and weighed about 100 tons (90.7 tonnes), dwarfing modern great white sharks.

Just as ancient organisms once covered the surface of Earth, their fossils cover the planet today. Many dig sites around the world are open to the public, and some allow visitors to dig for their own fossils—and sometimes even keep them.

The greatest number and variety of fossils are found in deserts and badlands—areas of heavy erosion and few plants.

GROUND SLOTH CLAW

NASH DINOSAUR TRACK SITE

For just a few dollars per person, you can visit the Massachusetts valley where a 12-year-old boy found the first North American dinosaur tracks while plowing a field. For a bit more money, you can take home a set of dinosaur footprints.

THE INSIDE SCOOP ON DIG SITES

18

THE WYOMING DINOSAUR CENTER

This park boasts some of the most fossil-rich strata in the world. Adults and kids alike can participate in a Dig for a Day program in search of leg bones, tailbones, ribs, claws, or full skeletons. Lucky hunters who find fossils will learn how to preserve them, and the fossils will be kept for future study. Even if you don't get to keep your fossil, you don't lose your bragging rights. Your name and the facts about your find will be noted in the museum's records.

PATAGONIA, SOUTHERN ARGENTINA

Thanks to erosion, scientists recently discovered their very own Jurassic Park, a vast expanse of ancient plants, marine creatures, and dinosaurs that once thrived there. "No other place in the world contains the same amount and **diversity** of Jurassic fossils," one scientist said.

THE MAMMOTH SITE OF SOUTH DAKOTA

Woolly mammoths once found this active paleontological dig site to die for. So far, the remains of sixty-one mammoths have been found there as scientists continue to search for more fossils. The exhibit hall features full-size replicas of mammoths and ancient species of bear.

19

You don't have to trek across the country or around the world to find fossils. You can find them in many common places all around you. Some of the best places to look include creek beds, in layers of sedimentary rock, along beaches, in deserts, or along rivers. Many fossils are also found in national parks, where you can drop by a visitor's center to view a map or ask for help. Or consider tagging along on a hunt with a local paleontology club.

Look for exposed rock, such as along cliffs or on shores, and be alert to details such as regular lines, spirals, or changes in texture or color. Be ready to search the ground on your hands and knees using a magnifying glass to study any specimens you find. If you are lucky enough to find a fossil, remember to leave it behind for the next lucky fossil hunter!

SAFETY FIRST!

When fossil hunting, always travel in a group led by an adult, and be aware of dangers around you. Stay away from steep edges, and be careful handling sharp rock. If your search could take you in a cellphone dead zone, carry walkie-talkies to stay in touch with your fellow fossil hunters.

THE FOSSILS AROUND YOU

ROCK-HARD FACT

Before you go, make yourself familiar with the five most common fossils, all once found within the sea. Being a good study will come in handy when you put your fossil-finding skills to the test!

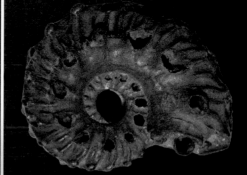

AMMONOID

BRACHIOPODS

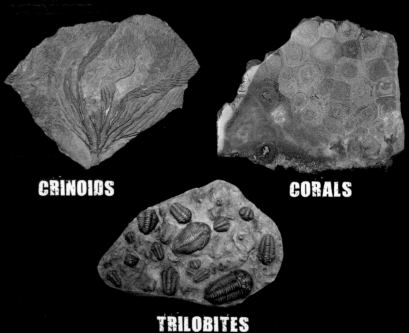

CRINOIDS

CORALS

TRILOBITES

Rocks, ice, and resin tell of a strange world that once was. These ancient plants and animals preserved within the fossil record are forever gone—or are they?

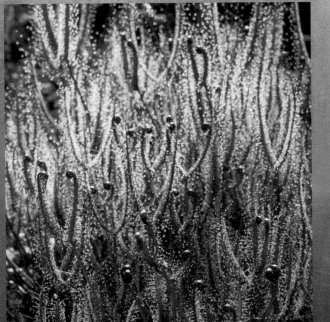

MEAT-EATING PLANTS

While searching a Russian amber mine, scientists found preserved leaves of meat-eating leaves that trapped prey in long, sticky hairs. The plant is an ancient cousin of a modern plant that traps prey later eaten by an insect, whose droppings nourish the plant. So which is worse—meat eating or dung eating? You decide.

A CLOSER LOOK: ANCIENT PLANTS AND LAND ANIMALS

BEAR-DOGS

A fierce hunter, this long-snouted animal that could measure more than 8 ft. (2.5 m) long could easily take down large prey—like the ancient rhino whose skeleton still bears a bear-dog's tooth marks. This is one type of dog that's best left in the past.

RABBITS' LONG-LOST COUSINS

It was the size of a rhino, with teeth—like knives and a bony head. Despite its huge size and big teeth, *Uintatherium* was a plant eater. Though it clearly lacked soft fur, long ears, and fluffy tails, the small-brained, hoofed mammal is somehow distantly related to rabbits.

TOWERING SLOTHS

The sloths of today are cute and cuddly (if they're not covered in moss, that is), and they only weigh about as much as a very well-fed pet cat. The sloths of the ancient world, however, were slightly less cute and cuddly. They stood a scary 10 ft. (3 m) tall, were just as long as they were tall, and weighed up to 2,205 lbs. (1,000 kg). But take heart: these monstrous mammals were plant eaters like their modern cousins.

ROCK-HARD FACT

Petrified wood is the most common petrified fossil. At the Petrified Forest National Park in Arizona—one of many places where such forests exist—visitors can see fossils of ancient trees that lived in a tropical forest. Fallen trees and branches were buried quickly under volcanic ash. Silica within the ash combined with minerals to replace the plant matter. Some petrified wood is so colorful and beautiful that it is used in jewelry.

FRANKENFLOWERS

Scientists claim to have brought back to life a plant that had been frozen to death under **tundra** 32,000 years ago. An ancient squirrel had stored the seeds in a burrow. Scientists found the seeds, took **cells** from them, and grew new plants from the cells, beating the record for the oldest plant brought back to life by 30,000 years.

Today, birdwatchers don binoculars to watch for favorite species. Some, like the eagle, are fierce hunters. Some, like the hummingbird, are no bigger than a pinkie. Some are rare and seldom seen, and some make wonderful pets. But in ancient days, their terrifying ancestors ruled the skies.

EUDIMORPHODON

ROCK-HARD FACT

In 2014, scientists discovered a new species of **pterosaur** with a crest on its jaw that looked like a throat pouch found on the modern pelican. The creature is called *Ikrandraco Avatar* because it resembles the Ikran creature from the popular movie *Avatar*. Scientists believe the creature skimmed freshwater lakes for small fish like many other pterosaurs.

A CLOSER LOOK: ANCIENT FLYING CREATURES

PTERANODON

KRYPTODRAKON

DIMORPHODON

THALASSODROMEUS

QUETZALCOATLUS

WINGED AND TOOTHLESS

With a wingspan of 18 ft. (5.6 m) and at 6 ft. (1.8 m) tall, pteranodon was a scary sight to behold. But it was true to its name, which means "winged and toothless." It likely ate small sea creatures or munched on the carcasses of dead land animals. A huge crest on its head probably helped balance out the weight of its long beak.

FAST AND FREAKY

Imagine, if you can, a flying reptile as tall as a giraffe and with the wingspan of a fighter jet, and you have *Quetzalcoatlus*. Scientists believe this incredible and somewhat scary reptile soared the skies at about 67 mph (108 kmh) on wings 39 ft. (12 m) across. These ancient predators are considered the largest flying animal that ever lived.

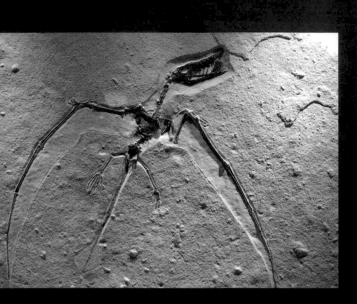

A NEW BUT OLD FIND

Scientists in China recently found the great-granddaddy of all pterosaurs in what's called a "dinosaur death pit" where prehistoric creatures sank to their deaths in quicksand. Unlike other pterosaurs, the *Kryptodrakon*—a name that means "hidden serpent"—lived inland, away from the oceans where its relatives hunted. Scientists believe the early pterosaur will help them understand how flying reptiles adapted.

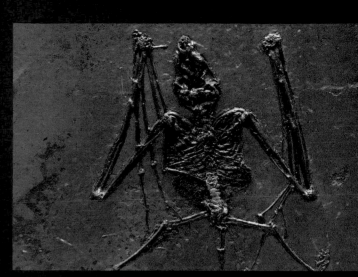

FUZZY AND CUTE

Scientists in China discovered the fossil of a small pterosaur with a 3.2-ft. (1-m) wingspan, claws, and what looked like fuzz. The fuzz, which turned out to be a fiber unlike hair or feathers, makes *Jeholopterus* a unique find. The insect-eating reptile had a protective covering over its claws, showing it could easily have won a tree climbing contest.

Ancient skies weren't the only place filled with terrifying sights. Ancient oceans were filled with scary creatures, including some that could qualify as sea monsters. At least one of those creatures is still found today.

KING OF SURPRISE ATTACKS

Compared with *Tylosaurus*, *Nothosaurus* was small, measuring at only 13 ft. (4 m) long. But this fearsome hunter, with its needlelike teeth and lightning-fast speed, is believed to have caught its prey in sneak attacks.

A PREDATOR'S PREDATOR

As long as a bus at 45 ft. (14 m) long and boasting teeth upon teeth upon more teeth, *Tylosaurus* was the deadliest predator of the ancient seas. It used its long snout to sniff out dinner, which it ate whole, no matter how big. Even a **plesiosaur** like the Loch Ness Monster couldn't escape its deadly jaws.

A CLOSER LOOK: ANCIENT SEA CREATURES

THEN THERE'S THIS GUY

To give you an idea of just how scary *Kronosaurus* was, it was named for Kronos of Greek mythology, who ate his own children. Let's say the name fits. This guy was bad, the kind of bad that bad guys fear—because it ate them.

THE ONE THAT JUST WON'T GO AWAY

The modern sea creature that strikes the most fear in a swimmer's heart is one that predates dinosaurs—SHARKS! With their row upon row of sharp teeth, sharks are windows into Earth's ancient history. The cow shark—still around today—is among the oldest shark species.

When we think of dinosaurs, we often think of giant, sharp-toothed meat eaters that could only survive in tropical climates. In truth, dinosaurs were incredibly diverse.

JUST PLAIN BIG

Scientists in Southern Patagonia recently found the biggest dinosaur fossil ever found—an animal 85 ft. (26 m) long that weighed more than seven T. rex. Though *Dreadnoghtus*—a name that means "fear nothing"—had no predators, it could easily take down enemies with its massive 30-foot-long (9.1-meter-long) tail. However, Dread, as it's nicknamed, was a plant eater.

SANTIAGO ■

CHILE

A CLOSER LOOK: DINOSAURS— BIG AND REALLY SMALL

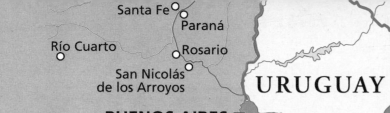

Santa Fe
Paraná
Río Cuarto
Rosario
San Nicolás
de los Arroyos
BUENOS AIRES
Lomas
de Zamora
La
Plata
MONTEVIDEO
ARGENTINA
URUGUAY
PATAGONIA
Bahía Blanca
Mar del Pl
Río Colorado
eral

TOWERING TERROR

This 6-ton (5.4-tonne), 40-foot-long (12.2-meter-long) predator known as *Mapusaurus* ate giant plant eaters such as brachiosaurs for lunch using its bladelike teeth to rip flesh off its prey. Worst of all, many fossils of this killer dino were found in one place, telling scientists it probably hunted in packs. The bones were found in Argentina.

A WANNA-BE MOVIE STAR

In 2005, a Canadian man noticed a snout sticking out from a cliff along a river. That snout turned out to be a new species of horned dinosaur, nicknamed Hellboy for its likeness to the popular movie character. A plant eater and cousin of Triceratops, this dino likely used its fancy frills in combat or to attract a mate. The fossil is on display at the Royal Tyrell Museum of Paleontology in Canada.

BIG ON CUTENESS

Only the size of a chicken, the big-eyed **biped** *Lesothosaurus* could have been the cutest and cuddliest of the dino realm. It ate low-lying plants using its beaked mouth while remaining on the lookout for predators. Its long, strong legs, hollow bones, and clawed feet would have helped it make a quick getaway.

A BOY NAMED SUE

T. rex ranks highest on the mega-scary meter, and the 13-foot-tall (4-meter-tall), 45-foot-long (13.7-meter-long) fossil named Sue—actually believed to be a male—is the biggest and best-preserved T. rex fossil of all. The fossil, which has a 600-lb. (272-kg) skull, was found in 1990 in South Dakota and is on display at the Field Museum in Chicago—if you're brave enough to go see it.

ROCK-HARD FACT

Some of the most amazing fossils are found by accident. That's the case with a 2011 discovery by a Canadian work-machine operator who bumped into something unusually hard while excavating. That something turned out to be the best-preserved nodosaur fossil ever found. The massive, armored plant eater was swept out to sea and petrified by rapid underwater burial, preserving its plates and some skin.

States choose symbols to represent them—flags, birds, and flowers, for example. Add fossils—yes, fossils—to that list. For most states, the choice of official fossil has resulted from a hard-fought battle waged by kids, teachers, or people in government.

STRANGE-BUT-TRUE STORIES: OFFICIAL STATE FOSSILS

TENNESSEE: PTEROTRIGONIA

University of Tennessee students and a professor had a mission. They wanted to increase public awareness of geology and paleontology, as well as the protection of the state's natural resources. Their mascot: an extinct sea creature named Pterotrigonia commonly found in Tennessee, part of which was once covered by an ocean. The creature, nicknamed Ptero, is considered the state's "spokesfossil."

ILLINOIS: THE TULLY MONSTER

In 1955, an amateur fossil hunter named Francis Tully made a strange and amazing find while searching through some piles of shale in Illinois. Two rocks opened, revealing a bizarre creature that looked like a fat worm with a lobster-claw tail. Scientists finally identified it as an ancestor of the modern lamprey, a blood-sucking fish that looks like an eel. Dubbed the Tully Monster, it has earned its place as state fossil.

CALIFORNIA: THE SABER-TOOTHED CAT

California's politicians were divided about what the state fossil should be. Should it be the extinct sea creature the trilobite, making California's state fossil the nation's oldest state fossil, or should it be the saber-toothed cat, a creature commonly found in Los Angeles' famous La Brea Tar Pits? Trilobite earned yawns from the state, making the scary and more exciting saber-toothed cat the all-around favorite and state symbol.

WASHINGTON, DC: CAPITALOSAURUS

OK, so Washington, DC, is a district and not a state—yet—but that hasn't stopped it from proudly backing an official fossil, *Capitalosaurus*. The only bones ever found of the prehistoric creature were unearthed in 1911 during construction in the nation's capital. The fossil has inspired a song ("Them Dino Bones"), a street sign, and even a Capitalosaurus Day each January in honor of its discovery. There's just one little problem: the jury is out on whether the beloved dino ever actually existed.

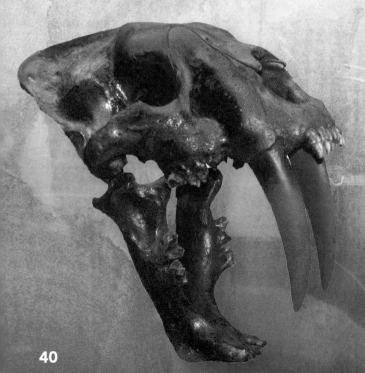

TEXAS: PALUXYSAURUS JONESI

In a display of Texas pride, the state wanted a locally found dinosaur to represent it. So in 1997, the state named *Brachiosaurus* as its state symbol, only to find out a decade later that the bones and trace fossils found in North and Central Texas actually belonged to another species. The 20-ton (18-tonne) *Paluxysaurus* is named for the Paluxy River and town by the same name, as well as the Jones Ranch, where the fossils were found.

All fossils are special, but some have rocked the scientific world by capturing a rare moment that shows how prehistoric creatures lived—or how they died.

Other finds have changed the way scientists view prehistoric life. Here are a few stars of the fossil world.

LIFE IN A HERD

In 1947, a pile of Coelophysis bones found in New Mexico changed the way paleontologists viewed **theropods** and large-scale dinosaur deaths. The bone pile showed scientists that some theropods lived in herds and that flash floods often wiped out dinosaurs of all kinds by the droves.

COELOPHYSIS

GREATEST FOSSIL FINDS

MEGALOSAURUS

THE BEAST OF THE EAST

Most dinosaurs found in the United States are found in the west. But the Hadrosaur preferred life on the East Coast—in New Jersey, to be exact. Discovered in 1858, the duck-billed plant eater was the first dinosaur fossil found in the United States and the first to be displayed in a museum. The dinosaur is so important to New Jersey's history that its image can be found in a stained glass window of the statehouse.

FIRST TO BE NAMED

Megalosaurus earned its name, which means "great lizard," in 1824, 18 years before the term *dinosaur* was even invented, making it the first named dinosaur. Just as it took scientists a while to figure out exactly what they were dealing with, it also took them a while to understand what Megalosaurus' fossils showed them. What was first thought to be a 50-foot-long (15.25-meter-long), four-footed lizard is now known to be a 20-foot-long (6-meter-long) biped, walking on only two feet.

HADROSAUR

Some of the greatest fossil finds have actually been frauds discovered after years of trickery or after careful investigation at the hands of a sleuth.

Perhaps the tricksters wanted to have some fun with scientists. Perhaps they wanted some excitement. No one may ever know their reasons—or even their identities.

PILTDOWN MAN

In 1912, scientists in England believed they had found the missing link—the creature that showed men evolved from apes. They called their find the Piltdown Man. They continued to believe that for 40 years, until radiometric dating and other tests showed the bone pieces didn't fit together. And no wonder they didn't: part of the fossil was from a human, and part was from an ape. The case remains a whodunnit, with even Sir Arthur Conan Doyle, author of the Sherlock Holmes series, as a suspect.

GREATEST FOSSIL FRAUDS

THE BERINGER HOAX

When 18th-century doctor named Johann Beringer took his students to a dig site, he was thrilled to find the motherlode of fossils: scenes of birds, bees, snakes, lizards, and plants. He even wrote a book about his find, only to discover the fossils were all the product of a cruel joke.

CARDIFF GIANT

The 10-foot-long (3-meter-long) Cardiff Giant of New York is often called America's biggest hoax and was a mean-spirited one at that. The so-called petrified giant was created by a businessman who collected up to $20,000 from people who came to see it in the 1860s, right around the time fossils became popular. The famous fake remains on display at the Farmers' Museum in Cooperstown, NY.

FOSSILIZED FLY

For 70 years, Britain's Natural History Museum proudly displayed a fly fossilized in amber as an example of how that species had remain unchanged over millions of years. But along came a student of ancient insects who discovered the fly was actually carefully placed inside the amber using a technique borrowed from jewelers.

ADAPT
to change physically in order to become better suited to an environment

ANCESTOR
an early plant or animal from which later organisms evolved

ARTIFACT
something made by a human, usually long ago

BIPED
an animal that walks on two legs

CELL
the smallest working unit of an organism

CLIMATE
weather conditions in a certain area over a long period of time

COPROLITE
fossilized poo

CULTURE
beliefs, practices, and arts of a certain people group

DIVERSITY
variety of life forms

ECOSYSTEM
a group of organisms and their shared environment

ELEMENT
a substance found in nature that is in its simplest form

ENVIRONMENT
the area or conditions in which a plant or animal lives

EROSION
the process in which wind, water, and ice wear away rock over time

EXCAVATION
digging a hole or carefully removing earth to reveal what's below the surface

EXTINCT
no longer existing

FOSSIL
the remains or imprint of an ancient animal preserved in part or whole either as a result of petrification or through a cast or mold

GEOLOGIC
relating to the study of Earth's makeup and physical history

GEOLOGY
the study of Earth's makeup and physical history

GLOSSARY

MAMMAL
warm-blooded animal with skin or hair that gives birth to live young, which it feeds milk produced within its body

MARINE
of, in, or made by the sea

MINERAL
a hard material from which rocks and gems are made that is found in nature and is not made of living things

ORGANISM
a life form, whether a plant, animal, or single-celled creature

PALEONTOLOGIST
a scientist who studies fossilized plants and animals

PALEOSCATOLOGIST
a paleontologist who studies fossilized poo

PETRIFIED
turned to stone

PLESIOSAUR
an extinct sea creature with paddlelike limbs, a long neck, and a small head

PREDATOR
a creature that feeds on other animals

PREY
an animal hunted by another animal for food

PTEROSAUR
a type of ancient flying reptile not related to dinosaurs

RADIATION
energy released through electromagnetic waves

REPTILE
a class of animal with dry, scaly skin that includes snakes, lizards, crocodiles, turtles, and tortoises

SEDIMENT
particles of matter carried by wind or water that settle on land or at the bottom of a water body, sometimes forming into rock

SEDIMENTARY
made from sediment deposited by wind or water

SPECIES
a group of similar organisms

SPECIMEN
a plant, animal, or mineral used for study or put on display

STRATA
layers of rock

THEROPOD
a meat-eating dinosaur that walked on two legs

TUNDRA
frozen subsoil

Written by C.J. McDonald
Designed by Brie Nagy

Copyright © 2018 Scholastic Inc.

Scholastic, Tangerine Press, and associated logos are trademarks and/or registered trademarks of Scholastic Inc.

Published by Tangerine Press,
an imprint of Scholastic Inc.
557 Broadway
New York, NY 10012

10 9 8 7 6 5 4 3 2 1

ISBN: 978-1-338-25662-8

Printed in Guangzhou, China

Scholastic UK Ltd., Euston House,
24 Eversholt Street, London NW1 1DB

tangerine Press®
an imprint of
SCHOLASTIC
scholastic.com